# It Could Be Verse

To Sybil
Love Light & laughter
Kitt~~Stapely~~

# It Could Be Verse

## An Anthology of Laughter Quotations

Collected by Kit Hammond Stapely
and Rhonda Blunden

Illustrations by Alice Gleadow

iUniverse, Inc.
New York  Lincoln  Shanghai

**It Could Be Verse**
**An Anthology of Laughter Quotations**

Copyright © 2007 by Kit Hammond Stapely

iUniverse books may be ordered through booksellers or by contacting:

iUniverse
2021 Pine Lake Road, Suite 100
Lincoln, NE 68512
www.iuniverse.com
1-800-Authors (1-800-288-4677)

Because of the dynamic nature of the Internet, any Web addresses or links contained in this book may have changed since publication and may no longer be valid.

ISBN: 978-0-595-43522-7 (pbk)
ISBN: 978-0-595-87848-2 (ebk)

Printed in the United States of America

# Disclaimers

The information, ideas, and suggestions in this book are not intended as a substitute for professional medical advice. Before following any suggestions contained in this book, you should consult your personal physician or mental health professional. Neither the author nor the publisher shall be liable or responsible for any loss or damage allegedly arising as a consequence of your use or application of any information or suggestions in this book.

All my research began with (to be sung to the tune of *Wonderful, wonderful Copenhagen*) wonderful, wonderful Wikipedia, the multilingual, web-based, free content encyclopaedia project. In the event that you would like to know more about anybody you encounter in these pages I recommend you start with Wikipedia, where the articles will direct you to more formal resources. Wikipedia is written collaboratively by volunteers from all around the world. With rare exceptions, its articles can be edited by anyone with access to the Internet, simply by clicking the *edit this page* link. The name Wikipedia is a portmanteau of the words *wiki* (a type of collaborative website) and *encyclopaedia*. Since its creation in 2001, Wikipedia has grown rapidly into one of the largest reference resources on the Internet.

In every article, links will guide the user to associated articles, often with additional information. Anyone is welcome to add information, cross-references or citations, as long as they do so within Wikipedia's editing policies and to an appropriate standard. There is no need to worry about accidentally damaging Wikipedia when adding or improving information, as other editors are always around to advise or correct obvious errors, and Wikipedia's software, known as MediaWiki, is carefully designed to allow easy reversal of editorial mistakes.

Because Wikipedia is an ongoing work to which, in principle, anybody can contribute, it differs from a paper-based reference source in important ways. In particular, older articles tend to be more comprehensive and balanced, while newer articles more frequently contain significant misinformation, non-encyclopaedic content, or vandalism. Users need to be aware of this to obtain valid information and avoid misinformation that has been recently added and not yet removed (see *Researching with Wikipedia* for more details). However, unlike a paper reference source, Wikipedia is continually updated, with the creation or updating of articles on topical events within seconds, minutes or hours, rather than months or years for printed encyclopaedias.

Wikipedia is a registered trademark of the non profit Wikimedia Foundation, which has created an entire family of free-content projects. On all of these projects, you are welcome to be bold and edit articles yourself, contributing knowledge as you see fit in a collaborative way.

If you have not done so, Wikipedia invites you to take a few moments to read What Wikipedia is (and is not), so that you have an understanding of how to consult or contribute to Wikipedia. http://en.wikipedia.org/wiki/Wikipedia:What_Wikipedia_is_not

# Dedication

Rhonda Blunden died in the spring of 2006 leaving behind a sparkling image of an extraordinary girl-woman who lived her life with joy and truth. She is profoundly missed by all who knew her and left the world a better place, if only because we all have a pattern of how it is possible to be full of knowledge, integrity, goodness and beauty but never—not for one instant—dull. In the same way she let me know her spirit was unchanged and unchanging by playing impish tricks on me in the days following her death I am sure that, wherever she is, she is gleefully aware of the fruition of the seed we planted together.

# Contents

# Acknowledgements

It is often said that writing a book is a lonely business. While that is undoubtedly true it is also true that, precisely because of the isolation, one is very dependant on the support, clarity, perspective, encouragement and interest of the people around you. Another truth is that without the invaluable help of certain wonderful people, this book would never have seen the light of day …

I must thank:
Patricia Neal for her generous and inspiring Foreword.

My parents for everything from their ready laughter all my life to their interest in the development of the book.

My husband, Simon, who has patiently borne my abstraction and tendency to say, "I'll be five minutes." only to emerge blinking from my study hours later. He has read through countless versions and still urged me on.

My lovely son, Alex, for his interest and encouragement.

The daughter of my heart, RonDeena, who has worked so generously to help the book be everything I hoped it might be.

Sally Sedgeman who inspired and encouraged me in the first place.

Annie Moore, for her enthusiasm and advice.

Alice Gleadow, whose wonderful drawings have brought the book to life and whose collaboration and style-development was one of the joys of this book.

Jill Corson, whose interest and enthusiasm kicked me over the line to getting real about the project.

David Avrick who shares his brilliance and friendship so liberally with me.

Caroline Stanley who crucially saw a seed in me to nurture when I had a tough time seeing it myself.

To the people contained within these pages. I have so enjoyed the discovery of the fascinating lives lived by all the amazing people whose thoughts expressed as quotes hooked me on finding out who they were and how they came by their opinions about the benefits of laughter.

Amanda Seyderhelm, Lesley Morrissey, Alex Greer and Simon Sholl for all they did.

For the stories I must acknowledge the contribution of that amazing phenomenon, Wikipedia. Wikipedia was invaluable in my research and a portion of the sales of every book will go to them to continue the unique contribution they make to the world.

*Last but not least, to Rhonda whose laughter still echoes through my mind.*

# Foreword

## By Patricia Neal

Kit's connections with my family go back to 1993 and, when I first met her, I was aware that she was mortally ill with cancer. Without revealing any particulars she was put through an unnecessary amount of cruelty and torment while she was fighting for her life. The only possible way she could have survived all that is to dig deep into her inner resources and effect a life transformation.

Since I have done very much the same thing—more than once—in my own life there is a kinship between us as, Phoenix-like, we have risen from the ashes of disaster with a strengthened belief in the power of laughter.

This book underlines the importance of laughter as a coping mechanism. It has always stood me in good stead and I hope the book will persuade you to use laughter liberally in your own trials.

Patricia Neal

# Introduction

This book has been written for those struggling with stressful situations.

It grew out of an idea I dreamed up with my colleague and dear friend Rhonda Blunden in 2002. We were both committed to reviving Laughter as the best and cheapest antidote to the spiralling stress of modern living. Everyone needs to laugh—even those who don't think they have a GSOH (good sense of humour). After all, we said, babies and children, who don't make, and certainly don't 'get' jokes, laugh up to 400 times a day.

We wanted to give to those people who most needed to laugh a book that was really accessible; that would seduce its readers into remembering to laugh when life was at its most challenging. Since we loved, used and collected 'Laughter Quotations' we decided to sort them into categories. The common bond between all the diverse individuals in this book is that they know the benefit of Laughter in the face of adversity.

In these pages you will find the brilliant, pithy insights of people from many cultures over the last 2,000-or so years; people who have suffered, struggled and survived and credit laughter as having been a healing part of the solution. You'll also find some of my own observations scattered here and there!

My desire is that you will find this book an accessible and uplifting collection of easy-to-absorb quotes. Maybe one or two will stick in your mind and help you to remember that it is not only OK to laugh through a rough patch—it is positively desirable. Perhaps you will wonder who it was that said those words that helped you and maybe that will prompt you to 'meet' some of these amazing people when you return to the book (as I hope you will, often).

I also hope that Alice Gleadow's wonderful images bring alive for you the stories and quotations from an assortment of always interesting, sometimes eminent, people.

On a personal note, it may be that you are saying to yourself, "OK but just how do I laugh with the sorrows and the pain that I have?" May I suggest that for books about the power of laughter you consult the bibliography on page 171 or visit my website www.miraclesdohappen.org.uk for some ideas.

*Kit Hammond Stapely*
*St Petroc, 2007*
Moored on the River Thames between
Kingston Bridge and Hampton Court Palace,
just outside London, England

# The Benefits of Laughter

## 65 Good Reasons to Laugh

1. Laughter is good for your health.
2. Laughter releases endorphins.
3. Laughter works as a form of exercise to flush out your lungs.
4. Laughter oxygenates the blood.
5. Laughter boosts the immune system.
6. Laughter creates the chemistry of happiness in your body.
7. Laughter is a universal language.
8. Laughter is a wonderful bond between people.
9. Laughter vaporises enmity and bad feeling between people.
10. Laughter cuts tyrants and bullies down to size.
11. Laughter relaxes all the muscles in the body.
12. Laughter makes your eyes shine.
13. Laughter reduces the harmful stress hormones in the blood.
14. Laughter reduces the effects of depression.
15. Laughter helps you to cope with the challenges of life.
16. Laughter builds self-confidence.
17. Laughter is an important social skill.
18. Laughter helps normalise blood pressure.
19. Laughter reduces—and sometimes eliminates—pain.
20. Laughter is an important coping mechanism.
21. Laughter is an important exercise for sedentary and bed-ridden people.
22. One minute of laughter = 10 minutes on a rowing machine. (Dr William Fry).
23. Laughter is contagious and can zip through a crowd uniting and energising.
24. Laughter promotes a sense of wellbeing.

25. The ability to laugh at oneself is one definition of a GSOH (Good Sense Of Humour).

26. Laughter helps us to think our way out of trouble.

27. Laughter diffuses tension.

28. Laughter refreshes us when we are out of hope and energy.

29. If you can laugh at any situation, however bad, you can survive it.

30. Laughter lightens any load.

31. Those who laugh a lot do not suffer from depression.

32. Laughter increases our H.Q. (Happiness Quotient).

33. Laughter relaxes the mind.

34. Laughter helps you make friends.

35. You need to express your laughter in order to be healthy and happy.

36. People who laugh easily and well, are popular and relaxed.

37. Laughing at your troubles is the fastest route to solving them.

38. Laughter helps us learn and remember.

39. Laughter is the release valve in the pressure cooker of stress.

40. Laughter helps us cope when life gets grim and serious.

41. Laughter transcends the barrier between ourselves and our spirituality.

42. Laughter dissolves fear.

43. Laughter works as well as any wonder drug and has no side effects.

44. Laughter with friends creates indelible memories.

45. Pain is part of life but, if you can laugh at it, suffering is optional.

46. However plain your features laughter creates magic and beauty.

47. The spirit of Laughter magnetically draws people to you.

48. Laughter conquers all adversity.

49. When you can laugh at the game of life you are automatically a winner.

50. Unless you can laugh at a situation you may drown in it.

51. Laughter paves the way for forgiveness.

52. Laughter changes mere Existence into Truly Living.

53. Laughter creates transcendence.

54. It is impossible to laugh wholeheartedly and hate at the same time.

55. Laughter fixes any fact or experience in the memory.

56. 30 minutes of mirthful Laughter can reduce serum cortisol by up to 87%.

57. Laughter in the face of trouble is universally admirable.

58. Laughter unlocks a frozen brain.

59. Laughter unlocks tense muscles.

60. Laughter neutralises fear.

61. Laughter dispels a bad atmosphere.

62. Laughter unites people in their humanity.

63. Laughter belongs to Youth so to laugh is to become Youthful again.

64. The ability to laugh at oneself is a certain cure for addiction.

65. Laughter by Jesters redeems Kings from the Abuse of Power.


## AND 5 THINGS THAT POISON LAUGHTER

1. Jeering Laughter makes both the laugher and the victim feel bad.

2. Laughter designed to exclude others shows mean-heartedness.

3. Laughter to deny remorse only compounds bad deeds.

4. Malicious Laughter is unforgivable.

5. Laughter at those in lowly positions shows a debased character.

Throughout the book you will find my thoughts contained in "think bubbles" like this one...

and you'll find the quotations in 'speech bubbles' like this one.

# LAUGH

## *To Feel Good*

## Sébastien Roch Nicolas Chamfort
## 1740–1794

French libertine, playwright, journalist, and revolutionary, Chamfort's career spanned the period leading up to and following the French Revolution. Called the 'wittiest of all moralists', he inspired a long line of thinkers.

Born Sébastien Roch Nicolas, the son of a grocer named Nicolas, he assumed the name of Chamfort. He had all the gifts: clever, handsome, strong, a witty conversationalist and an award-winning writer. He traded on his good looks and ready wit and was introduced at court where he was showered with honours and attention. His play was performed in front of Louis 16th and Marie Antoinette but, not liking the restrictions of court life, he left after a year.

The outbreak of the Revolution changed his life. He forgot his friends at court and threw himself fervently into the new movement. He became a street orator of revolutionary propaganda. When the Bastille was stormed he was among the first to enter but he was soon in trouble for his witty, sarcastic criticism of the bloody excesses of Marat and Robespierre and he himself was sent to prison.

Soon after his release, he was again threatened with arrest. Deciding that death was preferable to moral and physical restraint he made a horrendously botched suicide attempt. He began by shooting himself in the face. The pistol malfunctioned and even though he shot off his nose and part of his jaw he did not die. Next, he stabbed himself repeatedly in the neck with a paper cutter but upon failing to sever an artery, stabbed himself in the chest. He dictated to those who came to arrest him the declaration, *"I, Sébastien-Roch Nicolas Chamfort, hereby declare that I would prefer to die a free man rather than be re enslaved and perish in a prison,"* He signed it in his own blood but, tended to by a *gendarme* to whom he paid a crown a day, he did not die until the following year.

The most wasted of all days is that on which one has not laughed.

Sébastien Roch Nicolas Chamfort 1740–1794

# Henry Ward Beecher
## 1813–1887

A complex man, Congregationalist clergyman and social-reformer, Henry Beecher was America's foremost moral and spiritual leader around the Civil War. In 1875 he was accused of having an affair with the wife of his best friend, a scandal, which became one of the most famous trials of the nineteenth century.

His mother died when Henry was three. His father, an aggressive, reforming Congregationalist preacher who denounced intemperance, prostitution and slavery and forbade the celebration of either Christmas or the children's birthdays, does not sound a reassuring parent. Perhaps not surprisingly, Henry, although close to his older sister Harriet (Beecher Stowe, the author of *Uncle Tom's Cabin*), was bashful and mumbling as a child. Emotionally, he was close to a series of attractive young women during his life, but his wife, Eunice, the mother of his 10 children, was "unloved".

He clearly overcame his shyness because Mark Twain went to see Beecher in the pulpit and described him "sawing his arms in the air, howling sarcasms this way and that, discharging rockets of poetry and exploding mines of eloquence, halting now and then to stamp his foot three times in succession to emphasize a point".

During the Civil War, he raised funds to buy rifles to oppose slavery in Kansas and Nebraska, which became known as "Beecher's Bibles". Early in the war, Beecher pressed Lincoln to emancipate the slaves through a proclamation and went on a speaking tour in England to undermine support for the South by explaining the North's war aims. In 1865, near the end of the war, when the Stars and Stripes were again raised at Fort Sumter, Beecher was the main speaker.

The adultery trial began in January 1875, and ended in July when the jurors deliberated for six days but were unable to reach a verdict. He retained his influence although there is no doubt that the trial had sullied his reputation.

Despite this, his funeral procession—led by the black commander of a Garrison Post in Massachusetts and a former slave-owning Confederate general marching arm in arm—paid tribute to what Beecher helped accomplish.

Grim care, moroseness, anxiety—all this rust of life ought to be scoured off by the oil of mirth. Mirth is God's medicine.

Henry Ward Beecher 1813–1887

## Josh Billings
## 1818–1885

This was the pen name of the American humorist Henry Wheeler Shaw. He was, perhaps, the second most famous humour writer and lecturer in the United States in the second half of the 19th century after Mark Twain. His reputation has faded over the years.

Shaw was born in Lanesborough, Massachusetts and worked as a farmer, coal miner, explorer and auctioneer before he began making a living as a journalist and writer in Poughkeepsie NY in 1858. Under the pseudonym 'Josh Billings' he wrote in an informal voice full of the slang of the day, with often eccentric, phonetic spelling, dispensing wit and folksy common-sense wisdom.

His books include *Farmers' Allminax, Josh Billings' Sayings, Everybody's Friend*, and *Josh Billings' Trump Kards*. He toured, giving lectures of his writings, which were very popular with the audiences of the day. Billings died in Monterey, CA.

I love this image. It gives me a wonderful mental picture of people gasping and flapping about for the lack of laughter in their lives.

Genuine laughing is the vent of the soul, the nostrils of the heart, and it is just as necessary for health and happiness as spring water is for a trout.

Josh Billings 1818–1885

## Arina Isaacson

Arina is the Founder and former Artistic Director of the Clown School of San Francisco. She was also the creator of the original San Francisco Bay Area Hospital Clown Program and the Artistic director of Circus A La Mode, Inc., an after school circus program mainstreaming disabled and able-bodied children in the circus arts.

She has been a senior associate and principle trainer of Corporate Scenes, Inc. for fifteen years, consulting and coaching extensively with top management teams in the United States and worldwide. She is an internationally recognised director, actress and storyteller. As founder, artistic director and master teacher of the San Francisco School of Improvisation, Arina has worked with professionals from all walks of life for over twenty-five years. She holds a M.A. in Communications and Education from New York University.

People tell me they feel so much more available to life once they learn how to clown around. That's what being a clown is about ... it's about touching your soul and finally giving it room to laugh.

Arina Isaacson

## Barbara Johnson
## 1927–2007

Having lost one son in Vietnam and a second to a drunk driver, her third son disowned her to embrace a gay lifestyle. Instead of succumbing to grief and depression, Barbara Johnson founded Spatula Ministries to bring joy to other hurting parents.

She has guided millions of women through the tunnel of despair with her best-selling books, including *Plant a Geranium in Your Cranium, Living Somewhere Between Estrogen and Death*, and *Stick a Geranium in Your Hat and Be Happy*. She has sold more than 5 million books and she has delivered her comforting, humour-filled message of love across the USA as a featured speaker on the Women of Faith® tour. You can find out more about her at www.BarbaraSpatulaJohnson.com

Become
a child
again ...
Laugh!

Barbara Johnson 1927–2007

## Benjamin Jonson
## 1572–1637

English Renaissance dramatist, poet, actor and friend of Shakespeare, Jonson is best known for his plays *Volpone* and *The Alchemist* and his lyric poems. Much of what we know about him comes from his time as a guest of a man called Drummond who kept a record of all he said. Drummond described him as "a great lover and praiser of himself, a condemner and scorner of others". Since he scoffed at two apparent absurdities in Shakespeare's plays and said that he "wanted art", described his wife as "a shrew but honest" this assessment seems fair. He was jailed twice; once in Marshalsea Prison for a subversive play he wrote (he had an insatiable appetite for controversy) and once in Newgate for killing a man in a duel.

His popular playwriting led to a more prestigious career as a writer of masques for the Court of James I. On many of these projects he collaborated, not always peacefully, with the designer Inigo Jones. He lived in the tempestuous Tudor-Stuart era so his behaviour was not outlandish by the standards of the times and, despite his record, he received a royal pension of 100 marks (about £60) a year, identifying him as England's first Poet Laureate.

**Note:** In Elizabethan times, "Laugh and be fat," was considered a compliment. When only the prosperous were fat it implied that the speaker was wishing upon you abundance and prosperity.

Laugh, and be fat, sir, your penance is known.
They that love mirth, let them heartily drink,
'tis the only receipt to make sorrow sink.

Ben Jonson 1572–1637

# Herman Melville
## 1819–1891

The early novels of this American novelist, essayist and poet were popular, but his popularity declined during his lifetime. By his death he was almost forgotten, but *Moby Dick* was rediscovered in the 20th century as a literary masterpiece.

He was born in New York City, the third child of Allan and Maria Gansevoort Melvill (Maria would later add an 'e' to the name). His paternal grandfather, Major Thomas Melvill, was an honoured survivor of the Boston Tea Party. His maternal grandfather was General Peter Gansevoort, a hero of the battle of Saratoga. Melville relished his 'double revolutionary descent'. In 1832 his father died of a sudden illness and left his widow in genteel poverty, dependent upon her relatives.

Herman Melville's early career was as a sailor. Upon his return from the sea, in 1844, he published his experiences in the books *Typee, Omoo, Mardi, Redburn,* and *White Jacket*, achieving great success.

Melville married Elizabeth Shaw in 1847. He wrote his masterpiece, *Moby Dick* while living in their farmhouse in Pittsfield, but it was not successful. His writing career, once so promising, fizzled and his novella, *Billy Budd, Sailor*, remained in a tin can for 30 years. In 1924 it was discovered and published. Later it was made into an opera by Benjamin Britten, a play and a film by Peter Ustinov.

A good laugh is a mighty good thing, a rather too scarce a good thing.

Herman Melville 1819–1891

## William Makepeace Thackeray
## 1811–1863

A 19th century Anglo-Indian novelist, Thackeray is famous for his satirical works. In his earliest works, written under pseudonyms, his métier was merciless attacks on high society, military prowess, the institution of marriage, and hypocrisy. He wrote for the newly created *Punch* magazine, where he published *The Snob Papers*, later collected as *The Book of Snobs*. This work popularized the modern meaning of the word 'snob'.

In the Victorian era, his novels ranked second only to Dickens, but he is now much less read and is known almost exclusively as the author of *Vanity Fair* in which he managed to retain a light touch while satirizing whole swaths of humanity. It features his most memorable character, the engagingly roguish Becky Sharp. As a result, unlike Thackeray's other novels, it remains popular with the general reading public; is a standard fixture in university courses and has been repeatedly adapted for movies and television.

After the success of *Vanity Fair* he became so acclaimed for his satires on society that, taken up as an insider, he seemed to lose his zest for attacking it and his novels lost their keen edge.

His funeral was attended by seven thousand people; was buried in Kensal Green Cemetery in London and a memorial bust, sculpted by Marochetti, can be found in Westminster Abbey.

The world is a looking glass and it gives back to every man the reflection of his own face.
Frown at it and it will in turn look sourly upon you; laugh at it and it is a jolly kind companion.

William Makepeace Thackeray 1811–1863

## Mort Walker
## b.1923

Walker is an American comic artist best known for creating the newspaper comic strips *Beetle Bailey* and *Hi and Lois*. He was eleven when his first comic was published and aged twelve when he was first paid for one. In 1948, he went to New York to pursue his cartooning career. His first 200 cartoons were rejected but he was slowly gaining recognition.

His big break came with *Beetle Bailey* and another success followed with *Hi and Lois*. After more than 50 years in the business, Mort Walker still supervises the daily work at his studio, which also employs six of his children.

In his book *The Lexicon of Comicana*, Walker invented a cartoon vocabulary called *Symbolia*. For example, Walker coined the term *squeans* to describe the starbursts and little circles that appear around a cartoon's head to indicate intoxication and typographical symbols that stand for profanities, which appear in dialogue balloons in the place of actual dialogue.

Mort Walker has devoted his life to the business of lightening peoples' daily lives with cartoons and jokes—and is still at it today. I cherish this quote because it creates such a vivid image—who wants a heart that is so unused it is covered with cobwebs?

Laughter is the brush that sweeps away the cobwebs of the heart.

Mort Walker b.1923

# Thomas Carlyle
## 1795–1881

This Scottish-born mathematician is best known as a Victorian historian and essayist. His approach rejected analytic reasoning and advocated the more emotional and intuitive stances of the German thinkers like Richter and Goethe. His work was hugely influential during the Victorian era.

His parents expected him to become a preacher, but he lost his Christian faith; nevertheless, Calvinist values remained with him throughout his life. This combination of a religious temperament with loss of faith in traditional Christianity made his work appealing to those grappling with scientific and political changes that threatened the traditional social order.

Although he had such good words to say about humour, he wasn't markedly jolly. It was said that "It was very good of God to let Carlyle and his wife marry one another—by any other arrangement four people would have been unhappy instead of two!"

True humour springs
more from the heart
than from the head; it
is not contempt, its
essence is love.

Thomas Carlyle 1795–1881

# LAUGH

## *To Boost Your Brain Power*

## Saint Thomas Aquinas
## 1225–1274

St Thomas was an Italian philosopher and theologian who founded the Thomistic school of philosophy. Roman Catholics consider him the Church's greatest theologian and a model teacher for those studying for the priesthood. He is one of only 33 Doctors of the Church. His father was Count Landulf of Naples and, through his mother, he was related to a dynasty of Holy Roman Emperors.

At just five years old he began his education at the monastery. At university he came under the influence of the Dominicans, which was a revolutionary move in those days, and he fought his parents for years to join the order.

Although he was not considered fluent in speech, his written work was extraordinary. Aquinas was a big man with a dark complexion, large head and receding hairline. People described him as 'refined', 'affable and lovable', 'a pure person', 'humble, simple, peace-loving and much given to contemplation', 'moderate and a lover of poetry'. In arguments, he maintained self-control and winning over his opponents by his personality and great learning and made a remarkable impression on all who knew him.

His canonization happened despite his distinct lack of healings, miracles, stigmata or even an impressive regime of self-mortification. This apparently remarkable occurrence is thought to be due to his outstanding written work—a triumph of scholarship over saintliness.

It is requisite for the relaxation of the mind that we make use, from time to time, of playful deeds and jokes.

St. Thomas Aquinas 1225–1274

## Clarence Seward Darrow
## 1857–1938

An Ohio-born American lawyer and leading member of the American Civil
Liberties Union, Clarence Darrow was the son of idealistic parents; Amirus, an
ardent abolitionist and Emily, an early women's rights advocate. Throughout his
career, Darrow was vigorously opposed to the death penalty. In more than 100
cases, he only lost one. It was his first murder and he defended Patrick Prendergast,
the 'mentally deranged drifter' who had confessed to murdering Chicago mayor
Carter Harrison. Darrow's 'insanity defence' failed and Prendergast was executed
the same year.

He had little formal education, a keen intellect and an unassuming appearance
but Darrow was famous for moving juries and even judges to tears with his eloquence. A master of oratory, he often used poetry in his summations. When he
defended the teenagers Leopold and Loeb for the (very unsympathetic!) crime of
thrill killing, tears were streaming down the cheeks of the Judge as he ended his
lengthy address. He remains notable for the wit, compassion, and agnosticism
that made him one of the most famous American lawyers and civil libertarians.

If you lose the power to laugh,
you lose the power to think.

Clarence Darrow 1857–1938

# Charles Robert Darwin
## 1809–1882

An English naturalist famous for his theory, *The Origin of the Species*, in which he showed that all species of life have evolved over time through the process of natural selection. This was accepted as fact by the scientific community as well as the general public within his lifetime. His theory of natural selection became the accepted explanation of the process of evolution in the 1930s and formed the basis of modern evolutionary theory. His work and discoveries provide a logical explanation for the diversity of life on our planet and remain the foundation for contemporary work.

He was a tireless investigator of the world around him and a prolific writer of his findings. His best-known books include The Origin of the Species, The Descent of Man, and Selection in Relation to Sex, followed by The Expression of the Emotions in Man and Animals. His research on plants was published in a series of books, and in his final book, he examined earthworms and their effect on soil.

He is buried in Westminster Abbey in recognition of his eminence as a naturalist.

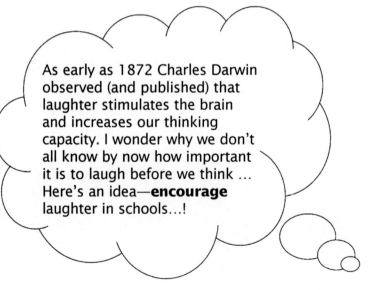

As early as 1872 Charles Darwin observed (and published) that laughter stimulates the brain and increases our thinking capacity. I wonder why we don't all know by now how important it is to laugh before we think … Here's an idea—**encourage** laughter in schools…!

(When we laugh) ... the brain being stimulated by the increased flow of blood, reacts on the mental powers.

Charles Robert Darwin 1809–1882

## Horace (Quintus Horatius Flacus)
## 65 BC–8 BC

Horace was a leading Roman lyric poet during the time of Augustus, the Golden Age of Latin literature in the 1st century BC. He is best known for his *Odes*, a collection of short poems famous for their irony and refinement, Horace also published satires, letters, and epodes (Greek choral songs).

Following the assassination of Julius Caesar, Horace joined the army and fought as an officer at the Battle of Philippi under Brutus. He later claimed that he saved himself by throwing away his shield and fleeing. On his return to Italy he purchased a profitable lifetime appointment as a *scriba quaestorius*, an official of the Treasury, which allowed him to live comfortably and still write poetry.

He became a part of a literary circle and was introduced to Maecenas (a friend of the Emperor Augustus) who became his patron and gave him a farm. It's still there today and acts as a literary tourist attraction.

For a man learns more quickly and remembers more easily that which he laughs at, than that which he approves and reveres.

Horace 65 BC–8BC

## Martial (Marcus Valerius Martiali)
## 40 A.D–102 A.D

Martial was a Latin poet from Hispania. He was best known for the short, witty poems in which he cheerfully satirised city life and the scandalous activities of his acquaintances, while romanticising his Spanish provincial upbringing.

Martial wrote over a thousand epigrams, which bring to life the spectacle and brutality of daily life in imperial Rome, with which he was intimately connected. His sexual outlook was in line with contemporary standards and thus same-sex love is a recurrent topic.

Martial prided himself on disliking hypocrisy, cant, pedantry or affectation of any kind and, due to a distinctive lewdness, his work stakes a claim for him to be regarded as the original insult comic. However, he must have been good-hearted because Pliny the Younger, on hearing of his death, said of him, "He had as much good-nature as wit and pungency in his writings".

The lovely thing about Martial is that in his humorous mockery of his fellow citizens he brings his time, in many ways so distant to ours, much closer. It seems that even in those days people were often made to feel even more poorly by the ministrations of doctors—who, even then, were trailing hoards of students! And not only did they have insurance—they had insurance fraud too!

Eg: *"Tongilianus, you paid 200,000 sesterces for your house. An accident, too common in this city, destroyed it. You collected 1,000,000 sesterces. Now I ask you, doesn't it seem possible that you set fire to your own house, Tongilianus?"*

Of course, it probably sounded wittier if you knew who Tongilianus was!

Laugh if you are wise.

Martial 40 A.D–102 A.D

# LAUGH

*To Improve Your Looks*

## Petronius
## 27–66 A.D.

Roman writer of the Neronian age Petronius was a noted satirist. His sole surviving work, *The Satyricon*, is an entertaining and earthy tale told in a series of bawdy and satirical episodes set in imperial Rome. It is familiar from the 1969 film by Federico Fellini.

Petronius lived a dissolute life and conspicuously modelled decadently luxurious living. He was recklessly frank which, oddly, won him popularity and he became one of Nero's intimates. In the end jealousy arose, an accusation was made and, apparently, Petronius was compelled to commit suicide. True to form he modelled the Voluptuary's Suicide. He opened veins and had them bound up again, whilst he conversed wittily with friends. He then dined luxuriously and slept for some time.

It was 'the done thing' to flatter The Emperor in his will. Instead Petronius chose to write a detailed description of the imperial sexual excesses and sent it to Nero as a sealed document. This lack of customary respect is underscored by Pliny the Elder who remarked that just before his death Petronius wilfully destroyed a valuable vase to prevent its falling into Nero's hands.

Those Romans! It seems that committing suicide was the only honourable course if you upset the Emperor. I saw Fellini's Satyricon when I was a romantic, idealistic 19-year old—and was absolutely repelled by it! I am glad to overlay that lasting disgust with admiration for his stylishly subversive method of complying with a custom that clearly enraged him. His stringent requirements of women sound sexist but, from all accounts, he demanded no less of men,

Outward beauty is not enough; to be attractive a woman must use words, wit, playfulness, sweet-talk, and laughter to transcend the gifts of nature.

Petronius 29–66 A.D

There isn't a face in the world that doesn't acquire a wonderful beauty when adorned with a whole-hearted smile or a laugh.

A smile is an
inexpensive way
to improve your
looks.

Anonymous

## Orison Swett Marden
## 1850–1924

Founder of *Success Magazine*, Marden is also considered to be the founder of the modern success movement in America. He bridged the gap between the old, narrow notions of success and the new, more comprehensive models made popular by best-selling authors such as Dale Carnegie, Norman Vincent Peale, and more recently, Stephen R. Covey, Anthony Robbins and Louise L. Hay.

The English writer Samual Smiles became Marden's first literary hero and inspired much that he wrote and accomplished. Smiles's *Self-Help* did much in the shaping of Marden's career. It became his ambition to become the Samual Smiles of America and there is little doubt that he achieved his ambition.

His book titles express an outlook of cheerful optimism and confidence. Marden was a definite and highly influential figure, whether consciously or not, in the outreach of New Thought ideas into the general culture of his time.

Joyfulness keeps the heart and face young.
A good laugh makes us better friends, with ourselves, and everybody around us.

Orison Swett Marden 1850–1924

## Victor Marie Hugo
## 1802–1885

Hugo is often identified as the greatest French poet. He was also a novelist, playwright, essayist, visual artist, statesman and human rights campaigner.

Victor Hugo is recognised as the most influential Realist writer of the 19th century. His best-known works are the novels *Les Misérables* (musical of the same name) and *Notre-Dame de Paris* (movie: *The Hunchback of Notre-Dame*). Among many volumes of poetry, *Les Contemplations* and *La Légende des Siècles* stand particularly high in critical esteem.

In my experience, people leave the rebellions of their youth behind them as soon they mature enough to acquire a mortgage! Hugo, although extremely conservative in his younger days moved to the political left as he grew older. He became a passionate supporter of Republicanism, which was then quite radical politics, and his work touches upon most of the political and social issues and artistic trends of his time.

Laughter is the sun that drives winter from the human face.

Victor Hugo 1802–1885

# LAUGH

## *To Sort Out What Really Matters*

In a balanced and healthy human being laughter re-adjusts every thing on every level and sets things right again. When we find we cannot laugh about an event we may be vulnerable to developing neuroses and post traumatic stress syndrome. The ability to laugh at life certainly does make the ride a lot less bumpy.

Laughter is the shock
absorber that eases the
jolts of life.

Unknown author

# William Hazlitt
## 1778–1830

An English writer remembered for his humanistic essays and literary criticism, Hazlitt is often regarded as the greatest English literary critic after Samuel Johnson for, it is said, his writings and remarks on Shakespeare's plays and characters are akin to Dr. Johnson's in their depth, insight, originality, and imagination.

When Hazlitt went to an exhibition of Italian old masters, he saw for the first time the paintings of Titian and Raphael and thought he could become a painter. "Till I was twenty I thought there was nothing in the world but books, when I began to paint I found there were two things, both difficult to do and worth doing; and I concluded that from that time there might be fifty." He dithered between being a writer and a painter until in the end he decided he would do better at writing and left a possible painting career in his wake.

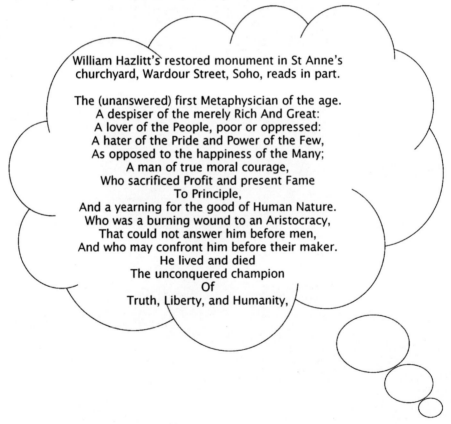

William Hazlitt's restored monument in St Anne's churchyard, Wardour Street, Soho, reads in part.

The (unanswered) first Metaphysician of the age.
A despiser of the merely Rich And Great:
A lover of the People, poor or oppressed:
A hater of the Pride and Power of the Few,
As opposed to the happiness of the Many;
A man of true moral courage,
Who sacrificed Profit and present Fame
To Principle,
And a yearning for the good of Human Nature.
Who was a burning wound to an Aristocracy,
That could not answer him before men,
And who may confront him before their maker.
He lived and died
The unconquered champion
Of
Truth, Liberty, and Humanity,

Man is the only animal that laughs and weeps; for he is the only animal that is struck with the difference between what things are and what they might have been.

William Hazlitt 1778–1830

## Kit Hammond Stapely
### b.1951

Born in Africa, and raised in England, I lived for 15 years in New York and now live on a boat on the River Thames in the beautiful English county of Surrey. Life begins at 40 they say; just weeks after my 40th birthday I was diagnosed with incurable cancer.

In hospital in 1997, having a 'last ditch' Stem Cell Transplant something happened that changed the whole direction of my life. My trusted inner voice told me that my Life Purpose is 'to increase the sum total of Love and Laughter on the Planet'. In 1998 when the cancer returned, I defied both my doctors and a disastrous life-situation by deciding not to die of the now aggressive cancer after all!

Laughter, jokes and silly playfulness have all played a big part in my survival and I credit them with making life a joy as well as helping me to scramble over the rough ground of cancer treatment and the unacceptable choices that it brings. I still prefer to use laughter as my Screen Saver, Default Setting and Reset Button.

As a general rule of thumb, toxic STRESS is anything we cannot laugh about.

Kit Hammond Stapely b.1951

## James Boswell, 9th Laird of Auchinleck
## 1740–1795

Boswell was a Scottish lawyer, diarist and author. The eldest son of a judge, Boswell is best known as the biographer of Samuel Johnson. His name has passed into the English language as a term (Boswellian) for a constant companion and observer. When they met, their first conversation went like this:

"Mr. Johnson, I do indeed come from Scotland, but I cannot help it."

"That, Sir, I find, is what a very great many of your countrymen cannot help."

The pair became friends almost immediately. Although Johnson denied any prejudice against the Scots, he once criticized Boswell for the Scottish habit of eating oats for breakfast: "In England we wouldn't think of eating oats; we only feed them to horses." To which Boswell replied: "Well, maybe that's why in England you have better horses and in Scotland we have better men."

When Boswell's *Life of Johnson* was published in 1791 it won him instant public admiration. It was revolutionary. For the first time, a book directly quoted conversations that Boswell had noted at the time, and included more personal and human details than readers were used to. The style of the time demanded a respectful and dry record of Johnson's public life; instead Boswell brought the complete man, vividly to life. According to some, it is still the greatest biography ever written, and perhaps Dr. Johnson's enduring fame is due, at least partly, to Boswell.

There is nothing worth the wear of winning, but laughter and the love of friends.

James Boswell 1740–1795

Such a neat, paradoxical way of reminding us that we often forget to laugh when our world seems to us a dark and scary place—which is when we most need to. Be an optimist in all things!

An optimist
laughs to
forget,
a pessimist
forgets to
laugh.

Anonymous

# LAUGH

*To Get Well*
*To Be Well*
*And*
*To Stay Well*

This maxim has been recognised for the last couple of thousand years—and not just in the Reader's Digest! Modern scientific studies are producing more and more stunning evidence of all the ways in which Laughter truly is the best medicine. A list of the benefits of laughter begins on page xvii.

Laughter is
the best
medicine

The Book of Proverbs,
The Bible

## Mark Twain
## 1835–1910

Mark Twain was the pen name of Samuel Langhorne Clemens, American humorist, satirist, writer and lecturer. His novels *Adventures of Huckleberry Finn* and *The Adventures of Tom Sawyer* are classics. Also famed for his quotations, he was friends with presidents, artists, leading industrialists, European royalty and enjoyed immense public popularity.

He was born in Missouri and his father died when he was eleven. The next year he became a printer's apprentice. Later he became a steamboat pilot, the third highest paying profession in America at the time, serving as a river pilot until the American Civil War broke out in 1861 and Mississippi river traffic ceased.

He began his writing career with light, humorous verse, but evolved into a chronicler of the vanities, hypocrisies and murderous acts of humanity.

The motivation behind Huckleberry Finn is the young boy's belief in following his own ideas of right and wrong even against the rules of society. Just as Huck ignores the rules to do what he considers just, Twain himself lived his life by his own lights. He claimed to have fallen in love with his wife Olivia at first sight and their happy marriage lasted 34 years.

The old man laughed loud and joyously, shook up the details of his anatomy from head to foot, and ended by saying that such a laugh was money in a man's pocket, because it cut down the doctor's bills like everything.

Mark Twain 1835–1910

# Peter Pindar
## 1738–1819

Peter Pindar is the pen name of Dr John Wolcot—a doctor, satirist and, at one time, clergyman. In 1767 he became physician to Sir William Trelawny, Governor of Jamaica, and induced the Governor to present him with a Church in the island and was ordained in 1769. When Sir William died in 1772, Wolcot came home and, abandoning the Church, resumed his medical career, and settled in practice at Truro.

In 1780 Wolcot went to London, and began writing satires under the name Peter Pindar using his remarkable wit, strong intelligence and ability to coin a phrase. His first targets, the members of the Royal Academy, were rather successful. Soon he was aiming higher and the King and Queen became his favourite subjects. Other targets included Boswell, the biographer of Johnson, and Bruce, the Abyssinian traveller. His satires amused his readers but his subjects were apparently cut to the quick.

It is nice to know that in other kinds of composition he showed an unexpected touch of gentleness and even tenderness. Much that he wrote has now lost all interest owing to the circumstances referred to being forgotten, but enough still retains its peculiar relish to account for his contemporary reputation.

Care to our coffin adds a nail,
no doubt; And every grin so
merry, draws one out.

Peter Pindar 1738–1819

## Friedrich Wilhelm Nietzsche
## 1844–1900

Nietzsche, (pronounced as knee-cha as far as I can gather), was a Prussian-born philosopher, who began his academic career as a philologist. He produced critiques of religion, morality, contemporary culture, philosophy and science. Nietzsche influenced existentialism, postmodernism, psychoanalysis, libertarianism and most subsequent thought.

Although Nietzsche became a professor at age 25, illness forced him to leave at age 34. With a pension he became an independent philosopher for ten years. His final eleven years were spent in asylums and Nietzsche's contemporaries largely overlooked him during his life, but he received recognition during the first half of the 20th century in German, French and British intellectual circles. Despite Nietzsche's professed opposition to anti-Semitism and German nationalism the German Nazi Party appropriated him as a forebear, which clouded his emerging reputation.

After World War II, Walter Kaufmann embarked on a sustained effort to rehabilitate Nietzsche's reputation in the English-speaking world and by the second half of the 20th century Nietzsche had achieved the status of a highly significant and influential figure in modern philosophy.

You must laugh ten times during the day, and be cheerful; otherwise your stomach, the father of affliction, will disturb you in the night.

Friedrich Wilhelm Nietzsche 1844–1900

**Patricia Neal**
**b.1926**

Patricia Neal, who won the Best Actress Academy Award for her performance in *Hud* with Paul Newman, grew up in Knoxville, Tennessee. She studied drama at Northwestern University, then appeared on Broadway and won the first ever Tony Award for *Another Part of the Forest*. In 1949 she made her film debut in *John Loves Mary* and also made *The Fountainhead* with Gary Cooper.

Neal married British writer Roald Dahl and produced five children: Olivia (deceased), Tessa, Theo, Ophelia and Lucy. While pregnant with Lucy, Neal had a series of three very severe strokes and was in a coma for three weeks. Roald directed her astonishing and legendary rehabilitation and she learned to walk and talk again. (They divorced in November 1983 after his affair with her friend, Felicity Crosland).

Following her rehabilitation she returned to the big screen. Her film credits include *The Breaking Point, The Day the Earth Stood Still, Operation Pacific, A Face in the Crowd* and *Breakfast At Tiffany's The Subject Was Roses* (Academy Award nomination). She starred as Olivia Walton in the pilot episode for *The Waltons* (Golden Globe Award). Her autobiography is, *As I Am* and *Patricia Neal: An Unquiet Life is* by Stephen Michael Shearer.

She is undeniably a Star who creates a hush just by entering a room and, unsurprisingly, her life continues to be full of interest and activity.

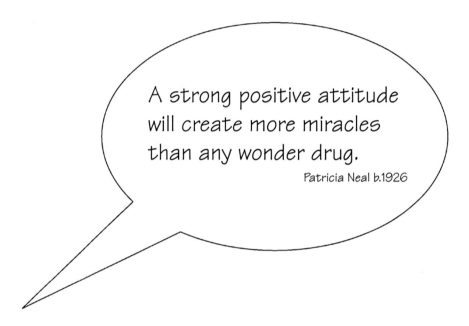

A strong positive attitude
will create more miracles
than any wonder drug.

Patricia Neal b.1926

## Abraham Lincoln
## 1809–1865

Despite humble origins, Lincoln was the 16th President of the United States. His father was an uneducated farmer in Kentucky—at that time considered the 'frontier'. In 1818, Lincoln's mother died aged just 34. Lincoln's father married again. Sarah Lincoln, his new wife raised young Abraham like one of her own children.

His formal education consisted of about 18 months' of schooling from unofficial teachers. In effect he was self-educated, studying every book he could borrow. His favourite book was *The Life of George Washington*.

Lincoln began his political career in 1832, at age 23, and served four successive terms in the Illinois House of Representatives. He taught himself law and was admitted to the bar in 1837. In 1842 Lincoln married Mary Todd who came from a prominent slave-owning family in Kentucky although Lincoln himself was an outspoken opponent of the expansion of slavery.

His election to the Presidency helped preserve the United States since he assumed unprecedented powers during the Civil War and, wanting to re-unite the nation, took a moderate and healing view over Reconstruction.

Lincoln's assassination in 1865 at the age of 56 made him a martyr for many people. He ranks among the greatest presidents in US history. Lincoln is usually seen as a figure who personifies classical values of honesty and integrity, respect for the individual, minority rights and human freedom in general.

Why don't you laugh? With the fearful strain that is upon me night and day, if I did not laugh I should die, and you need this medicine as much as I do.

Abraham Lincoln 1809–1865

This means, of course, no **harmful** side effects. The beneficial side effects to laughter are almost too numerous to list. You will find some of the most striking on page xvii and page 167.

LAUGHTER
is the only
tranquilizer with
no side effects.

Graffiti

# Galen (Claudius Galenius of Pergamum)
## 129–201 AD

Galen was an ancient Greek medical visionary whose work dominated European medicine for over a thousand years. He lived and worked in Rome where he was a court physician to Emperor Marcus Aurelius and must have seemed to his contemporaries positively God-like. Since most of Galen's writings were also translated into Arabic, he is known and honoured in the Middle East as "Jalinos".

Born in the Greek city of Pergamum, (modern-day Bergama, Turkey but then part of the Roman Empire) the son of the wealthy architect Nicon, he had eclectic interests: agriculture, architecture, astronomy, astrology, philosophy; before finally concentrating on medicine. He performed many audacious operations, including brain and eye surgeries that were not tried again for almost two thousand years. For cataract surgery, he would insert a long needle-like instrument into the eye behind the lens; he would then pull the instrument back slightly to remove the cataract. The slightest slip could have caused permanent blindness.

Galen moved to Rome in 162. There he lectured, wrote extensively, and performed public demonstrations of his anatomical knowledge. He soon gained a reputation as an experienced physician and attracted many patients. Among them was the consul Flavius Boethius, who introduced him to the imperial court, where he became a physician to Emperor Marcus Aurelius. Despite being a member of the court, Galen reputedly shunned Latin, preferring to speak and write in his native Greek, which was actually quite popular in Rome.

Galen was an extraordinary doctor—maybe because he originally intended to be a philosopher and was thus trained to think in a wider frame! A practice he pioneered that we still use today is the taking of the pulse.

There is a wonderful story about Galen that shows he was adept at psychological remedy for illness. He was called to the ailing wife of a Roman aristocrat as her own doctor had failed to help her.

He'd heard gossip linking her to a well-known actor and while Galen was taking her pulse, he mentioned the actor's name. Her pulse quickened dramatically. Apparently, having noticed her agitation, Galen then whispered something to her that made her laugh.

That laugh began her cure. Such is the healing power of laughter ...

## Lord Byron George Gordon Noel Byron, 6th Baron Byron 1788–1824.

A legendary personality in the Europe of his day, Byron was a heroic figure, poet and satirist, famous for his writings and, like a rock star of his time, his lifestyle. The latter featured extravagant living, numerous love affairs, debts, separation and allegations of incest and sodomy.

His sexual exploits are legendary - boys, siblings, women of all classes - and he bragged that he had sex with 250 women in Venice in one year. In those days, in Britain, men could be forgiven for sexual misbehaviour, but only up to a point. He was way beyond that point and, before long he was forced to live abroad.

Byron's romantic technique was to fully possess the object of his his desire - right up until the moment he became bored. He was memorably described by Lady Caroline Lamb, who was devastated by Byron's treatment and abandonment of her, as "mad, bad and dangerous to know".

Byron was a regional leader of Italy's revolutionary organization the Carbonari in its struggle against Austria, and later went to fight against the Turks in the Greek War of Independence. He died of fever and exposure in the Greek struggle and is venerated in Greece as a national hero.

Always laugh when you can; it is cheap medicine. Merriment is a philosophy not well understood. It is the sunny side of existence.

Lord Byron 1788–1824

# LAUGH

*To Improve
Every Relationship in
Your Life*

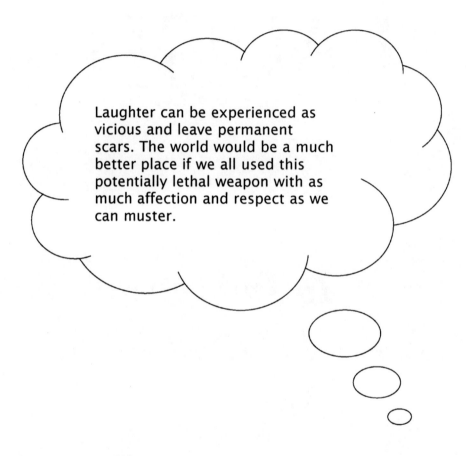

Laughter can be experienced as vicious and leave permanent scars. The world would be a much better place if we all used this potentially lethal weapon with as much affection and respect as we can muster.

When you laugh, be sure
to laugh at what people
do and not at what
people are.

Anonymous

I love this image, which deftly suggests that a smile in the eyes and on the lips is as warm and welcoming to those we encounter as a light in the window of a dwelling would be to a cold and hungry traveller.

A smile is the light in the window
that lets people know you're at home.

Anonymous

## Ambrose Gwinnett Bierce
## 1842–1914?

This American editorialist, journalist, short-story writer and satirist was best known for his *Devil's Dictionary*. As a critic he was reputed to have the power to make or break a writer's career. His simple, unsentimental style has sustained his popularity when many of his contemporaries have disappeared without trace.

In the American Civil War he fought at the Battle of Shiloh, a terrifying experience that became a later source for several short stories and the memoir *What I Saw of Shiloh*.

Bierce lived and wrote in England from 1872 to 1875, contributing to *Fun* magazine. In 1887, he was one of the first regular columnists and editorialists to be employed on William Randolph Hearst's newspaper, the *San Francisco Examiner*, eventually becoming one of the most influential and prolific writers on the West Coast—his *Collected Works* published in 1909 ran to twelve volumes.

The date of his death is generally given as '1914?' In 1913, in his 70s, he left for a tour of Civil War battlefields. He crossed into Mexico, which was in the throes of revolution and joined Pancho Villa's army as an observer. It is known that he participated in the battle of Tierra Blanca in that role. In one of his last letters, Bierce wrote, "Goodbye—if you hear of my being stood up against a Mexican stone wall and shot to rags please know that I think that a pretty good way to depart this life. It beats old age, disease or falling down the cellar stairs. To be a Gringo in Mexico—ah, that is euthanasia." After a last letter to a close friend he completely vanished. No investigations into his fate ever produced any results. The circumstances of his death remain a complete mystery.

Laughter—an interior convulsion, producing a distortion of the features and accompanied by inarticulate noises. It is infectious and, though intermittent, incurable.

Ambrose Bierce 1842–1914?

This is so true. Next time you are having one of those silly arguments when it is obvious that nobody's mind is about to be changed, try lightening up and having fun with the situation.

People who can agree on
what is funny can
usually agree on other
things.

Anonymous

## Jo Bunge
**b.1922**

This admirable, beautiful, wise, loving woman is my Mum and, whatever else I may or may not have had in life, I certainly won the lottery in the parent stakes! She demonstrated vividly a sense of fun and adventure and encouraged me in all my efforts to 'play it for laughs'. Still living zestfully in her eighties, she likes nothing better than a bit of fun and naughtiness and is always thrilled to collaborate in any mischief that might be going. Her spirit of playfulness lights up not only her own life but those around her as well.

You can forgive
someone an awful
lot if they make
you laugh.

Jo Bunge b.1922

## Russell Herman Conwell
## 1843–1925

American Baptist minister, lawyer, writer, and outstanding orator, Conwell's life was shaped by two great stories. The first occurred during the American Civil War when he, an unbeliever, served as a Captain in the Union Army. His ADC, a devoutly Christian 16-year old called Johnny Ring, idolized Conwell and was always with him. One of Ring's duties was to safeguard Conwell's sabre.

One day, when Conwell was away from the camp, the platoon was suddenly attacked and, forced into a hasty retreat, they burned a bridge to prevent pursuit. In a desperate attempt to save his Captain's sabre, Ring twice crossed the burning bridge. He saved the sword, but died of his burns. When Conwell heard of this he fainted and spent days in hysterical grief. He later converted to Christianity so as to be able to be with his friend in death.

As he told the story it was the love they shared that enabled him to accomplish what he did in his life. His crowning achievement was to be the founder and first president of Temple University in Philadelphia.

The second story is his lecture (and, eventually, book) Acres of Diamonds, which he delivered over 6.000 times around the world. It funded the construction of Temple University.

This little rhyme is widely quoted in Laughter circles and I love its message. What worried me is that the word 'virus' seems too modern for a man who died in 1925. So I looked it up ... apparently the word 'virus' has been in use since 1392 but it was not used in the sense of an agent that causes infectious diseases until 1728. You live and learn!

# Smile virus

by Russell H. Conwell

Smiling is infectious;
You catch it like the flu.
When someone smiled at me today,
I started smiling, too.
I passed around the corner
And someone saw my grin
When he smiled, I realized
I'd passed it on to him!
I thought about that smile
And then realized its worth,
A single smile, just like mine,
Could travel round the earth.
So, if you feel a smile begin,
Don't leave it undetected,
Let's start an epidemic quick,
And get the world infected!

This is a quote I love and use frequently. In a similar vein, I have a friend who leers at you and says, 'I want to give you something catching.' Just when you are wondering uneasily what he has in mind, he adds 'My smile.' But it isn't quite as sunnily quotable as this one!

If you see someone without a smile, give them one of yours!

Anonymous

## Dr Robert Holden

British Director and Founder of The Happiness Project, Robert is a pioneer in the field of Positive Psychology and Wellbeing. His pioneering work has been featured in the BBC TV *QED* documentary Called *How to be Happy* - now shown in 16 countries to over 30 million television viewers.

Robert holds a Ph.D. in the Psychology of Happiness. He has given public lectures worldwide and shared platforms with Deepak Chopra, Wayne Dyer, Patch Adams, Alan Cohen and Paul McKenna and has been featured on *Oprah*.

Laughter is a highly addictive, positive contagion: if somebody starts, it's very difficult to stop.

Robert Holden

## William James
## 1842–1910

A pioneering American psychologist and philosopher, James wrote influential books on the, then, young science of psychology. These included educational psychology, psychology of religious experience and mysticism, and the philosophy of pragmatism.

Born in New York City, son of Henry James, Sr., an independently wealthy and notoriously eccentric theologian, part of the literary and intellectual elites of his day. The intellectual brilliance of the James family milieu and its writing talents is remarkable. William James, with his younger brother Henry James (who became a prominent novelist) and sister Alice James (who is known for her posthumously published diary), received an eclectic trans-Atlantic education, developing fluency in both German and French languages along with a cosmopolitan character.

James knew a wide circle of writers and scholars during his life, including his godfather, Ralph Waldo Emerson; Oliver Wendell Holmes, Jr., Josiah Royce, Helen Keller, Mark Twain, H. G. Wells, G. K. Chesterton, Sigmund Freud, Gertrude Stein, and Carl Jung.

I think it's fascinating that William James and both his siblings achieved such notable success and fame. Of course, the fact that this tends to prove all my theories and misgivings about schools and education is purely co-incidental!

One hearty laugh together will bring enemies into a closer communion of heart than hours spent on both sides in inward wrestling with the mental demon of uncharitable feeling.

William James 1842–1910

# LAUGH

## *To Build Success*

## Robert Louis (Balfour) Stevenson
## 1850–1894

Stevenson was a British writer, essayist, poet, novelist and leading representative of Neo-romanticism in English literature. He was descended from three generations of distinguished lighthouse designers and engineers. However, his physical frailty (he had weak lungs) and interests inclined him to writing.

It was love at first sight when he met his wife and they were very happy but his health was never good. On the death of his father, in 1887, he felt free to follow the advice of his physician to try a complete change of climate. He started out with his mother and family for Colorado and in 1890 he bought land on a Samoan island.

He died suddenly within a few hours at the age of 44. The natives insisted on surrounding his body with a watch-guard during the night, and on bearing their 'Story Writer' several miles upon their shoulders to the top of a cliff overlooking the sea, where he was buried.

He was greatly admired by many authors, including G.K.Chesterton, Jorge Luis Borges, Ernest Hemingway, Rudyard Kipling and Vladimir Nabokov, but it is only recently that critics have begun to look beyond Stevenson's popularity and allow him his rightful place in literature's history.

The man is a success who has lived well, laughed often, and loved much; who has gained the respect of intelligent men and the love of children; who has filled his niche and accomplished his task; who leaves the world better than he found it, whether by an improved poppy, a perfect poem, or a rescued soul; who never lacked appreciation of earth's beauty or failed to express it; who looked for the best in others and gave the best he had.

Robert Louis Balfour Stevenson 1850–1894

## Will Rogers (William Penn Adair Rogers)
## 1879–1935

An iconic American comedian, humorist, social commentator, vaudeville performer and actor, Rogers' life bridged the gap between the America of the Wild West and the emerging America of the early 20th century. He was born in what would later become the state of Oklahoma on the Dog Iron Ranch in Indian Territory; both his parents had Cherokee blood.

With a 10th grade education and itchy feet he honed his roping skills in Argentina and South Africa. He was breaking horses for the British Army when he entered show business as a trick roper. On his return to the US he continued as a performer. His wry comments when he missed a trick went down so well he worked more jokes into his act.
He would appear on stage in his cowboy outfit, nonchalantly twirling his lasso, and say, "Well, what shall I talk about? I ain't got anything funny to say. All I know is what I read in the papers." He would then make jokes about what he had read in that day's newspapers. His act was a great success and he became a star of the Ziegfield's Follies. The rest, as they say, is (showbiz) history.

America couldn't get enough of Rogers' simple, upbeat 'take' on life which made them pause, think and laugh. He appeared in many silent films and over 21 feature films, was the nation's No. 1 movie box office draw in 1934 and hosted the 7th Annual Academy Awards Ceremony. He was the most widely read newspaper columnist and his half-hour radio show was the nation's most-listened-to weekly broadcast. An avid fan of aviation, Rogers was the first civilian to fly coast to coast on early airmail flights. On a sightseeing trip to Alaska with a world-renowned aviator, Wiley Post, the plane crashed killing both men.

We are all here for a spell; get all
the good laughs you can.

Will Rogers 1879–1935

# Katherine Mansfield
## 1888–1923

Kathleen Mansfield Beauchamp was born into a socially prominent family in Wellington, New Zealand. She moved to London in 1902, where she attended Queen's College. She is widely considered one of the best short story writers of her period. Mansfield proved ahead of her time in her adoration of Russian playwright Anton Chekhov and incorporated some of his themes and techniques into her writing. The fact that Mansfield died relatively young - of tuberculosis - only added to her legacy.

She was given to tempestuous up and down relationships and vivid contradictions - fiercely independent/desperately needy, boldly unconventional/excessively apologetic, ambitious/full of self-doubt. "For happiness and freedom", she wrote in her journal, "We must get rid of that bogey" (that love is the only thing in the world) and immediately went and fell in love with a young violinist. When that affair collapsed, she impulsively married a singing teacher, left him the day after the wedding and returned to the violinist. She became pregnant, and eventually had a stillborn child.

In 1912 she met and married John Middleton Murry, a student and editor of a literary journal for writing and art that was full of 'guts and bloodiness'. Even then she continued her lifelong pattern of partings and reconciliations. During one parting she made a daring trip to in the French war zone visit her lover, a bohemian writer. Eventually her tuberculosis caused her to shuttle between London and the French Riviera, which created a stock of vivid letters and journals that, posthumously, has garnered her yet another impressive literary reputation.

When we begin to take our failures non-seriously, it means we are ceasing to be afraid of them. It is of immense importance to learn to laugh at ourselves.

Katherine Mansfield 1888–1923

## John Fitzgerald Kennedy
## 1917–1963

35th president of the United States, Kennedy served from 1961 until his death in 1963. He is the only Roman Catholic to be elected president of the country. His assassination in Dallas was an epoch-defining moment. Lee Harvey Oswald, charged with the crime, was himself murdered, two days later, allegedly by Jack Ruby - before an Oswald trial could be convened. The Warren Commission concluded that Oswald had acted alone in killing the president. However, the House Select Committee on Assassinations, later, concluded that there may have been a conspiracy.

The first politician I ever noticed as a child was President Kennedy. He seemed young and joyous. He laughed and made jokes with such energy and verve that I was surprised to read later that he had been in chronic pain with a back problem. Such was his charisma that it is true to say that there was a movie star glamour that attended both him and his wife, Jackie, even before his dramatic death made them the stuff of legend. Today he is regarded as an icon of American hopes and aspirations to ever-new generations of Americans.

There are only three eternal
elements in the world:
God, human folly and laughter
and, since the first two pass all
comprehension, we must do what
we can with the third.
Old Arab Saying much enjoyed by and quoted by John F Kennedy 1917–1963

## Ralph Waldo Emerson
## 1803–1882

Born in Boston, Emerson was an American essayist, poet, and leader of the Transcendentalist movement in the early nineteenth century. His father, the Rev. William Emerson died when Ralph was eight having described him as 'a rather dull scholar'. This left his mother to bring up their five sons in poverty, including one with a mental handicap.

Ralph became a Unitarian minister in 1829. His brief career as a minister was marred by religious doubt and by his wife's death in 1831. He gradually drifted from the doctrines of his peers, and began to formulate the philosophy of Transcendentalism.

In 1835, he remarried and settled in Concord and with other like-minded intellectuals founded the Transcendental Club, which served as a centre for the movement. In 1836 his essay, Nature, expressing his beliefs, was published anonymously. In an 1838 speech at the Harvard Divinity School he stated that Jesus was a great man but he was not God. This outraged the establishment and shocked the whole Protestant community and he was denounced as an atheist and a poisoner of young minds. He made no reply himself, leaving his defence to others but by the mid-1880s his once radical beliefs had become standard Unitarian thought.

Compare his quote to that of Robert Louis Stevenson's (on page 99) and decide for yourself who influenced whom.

The definition of success: To laugh often and love much; to win the respect of intelligent persons and the affection of children; to earn the approbation of honest citizens and endure the betrayal of false friends; to appreciate beauty; to find the best in others; to give of one's self; to leave the world a bit better, whether by a healthy child, a garden patch or a redeemed social condition; to have played and laughed with enthusiasm and sung with exultation; to know even one life has breathed easier because you have lived—this is to have succeeded.

Ralph Waldo Emerson 1803–1882

## Andrew Carnegie
## 1835–1919

Carnegie was a Scottish-American Industrialist businessman, a major and widely respected philanthropist and the founder of the Carnegie Steel Company, which later became U.S. Steel. Best remembered for Carnegie Hall on W. 57$^{th}$ Street in New York City.

He was a poor boy with fierce ambition, a pleasant personality, and a devotion to both hard work and self-improvement. He started as a telegrapher. He built wealth as a bond salesman raising money in Europe for American enterprises and by the 1860's he had investments in railroads, railroad sleeping cars, as well as bridges and oil derricks.

Steel was where he made his fortune. In the 1870's he founded the Carnegie Steel Company, a step which made his name as a 'Captain of Industry'. By the 1890's the company was the largest and most profitable industrial enterprise in the world. He sold it to J.P. Morgan's U.S, Steel in 1901 and devoted the remainder of his life to large-scale philanthropy, giving away most of his riches, in Scotland, America, and worldwide, to fund the establishment of many libraries, schools, and universities. He also funded the internationally renowned concert hall, which inspired one of my favourite jokes:

> Q: *"Can you tell me how to get to Carnegie Hall?"*
> A:: *"Practise. Practise. Practise".*

There is little success where there is little laughter.

Andrew Carnegie 1835–1919

# LAUGH

## *To Confront Fear*

## Giacomo Leopardi
## 1798–1837

An Italian Count, poet, essayist, philosopher and philologist, Leopardi is generally considered to be among Italy's greatest poets and one of its greatest thinkers.

He had a sad and difficult life. His ill health as a child kept him housebound in a palazzo poisoned by the atmosphere generated by his reactionary father whose gambling addiction financially ruined the family and a despotic, cold religious fanatic of a mother obsessed with rebuilding the family fortunes.

These circumstances no doubt set him in the emotional state of anguished pessimism that dominated his life. He studied constantly to escape and burned out his already fragile constitution. It is comforting to think that laughter helped him to cope in the face of such relentless personal unhappiness.

One who has the courage to laugh is almost as much the master of the world as he who is ready to die.

Giacamo Leopardi 1798–1837

# René Descartes
## 1596–1650

Also known as Cartesius, Descartes was a noted French philosopher, mathematician and scientist. He is dubbed the 'Founder of Modern Philosophy' and the 'Father of Modern Mathematics'. He ranks as one of the most important and influential thinkers of modern times, and coined the phrase, "I think, therefore I am" (*"Je pense, donc je suis"*).

He was always frail, and, as an adult, he spent most of his mornings in bed, where he did his Thinking, musing on the dreams, which often brought him revelations. For good or bad, much of subsequent Western Philosophy is a reaction to his writings, which have been closely studied from his time down to the present day. Descartes was one of the key thinkers of the Scientific Revolution in the Western World. His influence in mathematics is also apparent; the Cartesian coordinate system used in plane geometry and algebra is named after him. In his latter years, Descartes went to Sweden to tutor Queen Christina in philosophy. Unfortunately, the Queen was an early riser and insisted on taking her lessons at 5:00 a.m. This regime did not suit Descartes' fragile health. He got pneumonia and died at the age of 54.

Your joy is your sorrow
unmasked. And the
self-same well from
which your laughter rises
was often-times filled
with your tears.

René Descartes 1596–1650

## Voltaire (François-Marie Arouet)
## 1694–1778

Voltaire (the pen name of François-Marie Arouet) was one of the most controversial and influential figures of his time. French enlightenment writer, essayist, deist and philosopher, he was known for his wit, philosophical writings, and defence of civil liberties. He was an outspoken supporter of social reform despite strict censorship laws in France and harsh penalties for those who broke them.

In 1726 he was exiled to England without trial. This may have been a mistake as the ideas and experiences he met during his exile influenced him for the rest of his life. He was impressed by England's constitutional monarchy and the country's support of the freedoms of speech and religion. Influenced by several neoclassical writers of the age, he developed an interest in earlier English literature, especially the works of Shakespeare. He returned to Paris in 1729 where he published his views on English attitudes towards government and literature; these letters met great controversy in France. Copies of the document were burnt and Voltaire was forced to leave Paris.

He spent the next 15 years as the lover of the Marquise du Chatelet. They collected over 21,000 books, an enormous number for their time and together they studied these books and performed scientific experiments.

After the death of the Marquise, Voltaire moved to Berlin to join Frederick the Great, a close friend and admirer, who gave him a salary of 20,000 francs a year. However, when Voltaire wrote a document mocking the president of the Berlin Academy of Science it angered Frederick, who had Voltaire arrested and all copies of the document burned. Louis XV banned him from Paris, so instead he turned to Geneva where he bought a large estate and lived there until his death, which actually occurred on a visit to Paris.

God is a
comedian
playing to an
audience too
afraid to laugh.
Voltaire 1694–1778

# LAUGH

*To Measure Character*

# Plato
## 427–327 B.C.

Plato, a Greek philosopher, was considered the inventor of philosophic argument. The youngest son of a famous, wealthy and long-established Athens family, his original name was Aristocles. 'Plato' (which translates roughly 'the broad') was a nickname. Who knows if it was because of his shoulders, wrestling training, the scope of his mind, the size of his forehead or even an ironic way of calling him 'thick' because he so obviously wasn't?

Plato's uncle was a close friend of Socrates so he probably knew Socrates from an early age. He was in military service from 409 BC to 404 BC but he wanted a political career rather than a military one. However, Athenian political life, in particular Socrates' execution in 399 BC affected him strongly and he decided he would have nothing more to do with politics in Athens.

He travelled in Egypt, where he discovered a water clock and brought it back to Greece, as well as Sicily and Italy. In Italy he learned about Pythagoras and the value of mathematics. He believed in absolute truth and he became convinced that mathematics was the way to figure out those truths.

About 387 BC, Plato returned to Athens and founded his Academy on land that had belonged to a man called Academos. (This is how the name 'Academy' was formed). The Academy was an institution devoted to research and instruction in philosophy and the sciences and made many radical scientific discoveries. Plato, himself, made no important discoveries in mathematics but he played a vital role in developing a purer approach to mathematics. Plato presided over it from 387 BC until his death (aged 100) in 347 BC. Plato's Academy flourished until 529 AD when it was closed down by the Christian Emperor, Justinian, who claimed it was a pagan establishment. Having survived for 900 years it is the longest surviving university known.

Plato also invented the ideal of a platonic relationship. For years, being rather a fan of 'all that cheap physical stuff' I thought this a very uninteresting idea. His lovely insightful quote puts it all in a very different light.

You can discover more about a person in an hour of play than in a year of conversation.

Plato 427–347 B.C.

## Ella Wheeler Wilcox
## 1850–1919

American author and poet, Ella's work is best known for the oft-quoted couplet from her three-versed poem, *Solitude*: "Laugh and the world laughs with you/Weep and you weep alone." Her autobiography, *The Worlds and I* was published in 1918 shortly before her death.

She was born on a farm in Wisconsin, the youngest of four children and started writing poetry at a very early age. Her reputation was established before she was 20. She married Robert Wilcox when she was 28 and they had one child, who died shortly after birth. Not long after their marriage they both became interested in theosophy. They promised each other that whoever died first would communicate with the other. Robert Wilcox died in 1916, after over thirty years of marriage. She was overcome with grief, which became more intense as weeks went by without any message from him.

Unable to understand why she had had no message, she went to California to see Max Heindel. "In talking with Max Heindel, the leader of the Rosicrucian Philosophy in California, he made very clear to me the effect of intense grief. Mr. Heindel assured me that I would come in touch with the spirit of my husband when I learned to control my sorrow. I replied that it seemed strange to me that an omnipotent God could not send a flash of his light into a suffering soul to bring it conviction when most needed. 'Did you ever stand beside a clear pool of water,' asked Mr. Heindel, 'and see the trees and skies repeated therein?' And did you ever cast a stone into that pool and see it clouded and turmoiled, so it gave no reflection? Yet the skies and trees were waiting above to be reflected when the waters grew calm. So God and your husband's spirit wait to show themselves to you when the turbulence of sorrow is quieted".

It is easy enough to be pleasant,
When life flows by like a song,
But the man worthwhile is one who will smile
When everything goes dead wrong.
For the test of the heart is trouble,
And it always comes with the years,
And the smile that is worth the praises of earth
Is the smile that shines through tears.

Ella Wheeler Wilcox 1850–1919

## P.T. (Phineas Taylor) Barnum
## 1810–1891

The American Showman is best remembered for founding the circus that was sold to Ringling Brothers (in 1907 for the price of US$400,000). This became Ringling Brothers and Barnum and Bailey Circus. The award-winning musical, *Barnum*, is based on his life and exploits.

There was more to Barnum; he wrote several books and his genius for marketing ensured that his autobiography was one his most successful methods of self-promotion. It was so popular that, by the end of the C19[th], the number of copies printed was second only to the number of copies of the New Testament printed in North America!

He built four mansions in Connecticut during his life and had a significant political career. Barnum was elected to the Connecticut legislature in 1865 as the Republican representative for Fairfield and served two terms. He spoke eloquently before the legislature in the debate over slavery saying notably, "A human soul is not to be trifled with. It may inhabit the body of a Chinaman, a Turk, an Arab or a Hottentot—it is still an immortal spirit!"

He served a one-year term as mayor of Bridgeport CT and worked vigorously to improve the city water supply, bring gas lighting to the streets, and strictly enforced liquor and prostitution laws. He was instrumental in starting Bridgeport Hospital and served as its first president.

Give me a man who laughs in earnest, as though it comes from the heart, and a hundred-to-one that is a whole-souled, liberal-minded and charitable fellow.

P.T. Barnum 1810–1891

## Jane Carlyle (née Welsh)
## 1801–1866

Jane was from Haddington, Scotland and married essayist Thomas Carlyle. She has been cited as the reason for his fame and fortune. She, herself, was a notable letter-writer, and in 1973 was described by G.B Tennyson as, "One of the rare Victorian wives who are of literary interest in their own right … to be remembered as one of the great letter writers (in some respects her husband's superior) of the nineteenth century is glory beyond the dreams of avarice."

Carlyle and Jane married in 1826, but the marriage was not happy. The letters between them show that although the couple had affection for each another their relationship involved many quarrels.

They became increasingly alienated and when Jane died unexpectedly Carlyle was plunged into despair. He wrote the self-accusatory *Reminiscences of Jane Welsh Carlyle*, which was published after his death by his self-chosen biographer, James Froude, who also revealed his belief that the marriage was unconsummated. This frankness was unheard of in the usually respectful biographies of the period. I like to think that Jane's quote means that she and her husband shared hearty laughter as well as the bitterness and misunderstandings.

No man who has once
heartily and wholly
laughed can be altogether
irreclaimably bad.

Jane Carlyle (nee Welsh) 1801–1866

## Fyodor Mikhailovich Dostoevsky
## 1821–1881

One of the greatest Russian writers [his works include *Crime and Punishment* and *The Brothers Karamazov*], Dostoevsky had a huge effect on 20th century world literature. His father, a retired military surgeon and a violent alcoholic, was a doctor at the Mariinsky Hospital for the Poor in one of the worst areas in Moscow amidst a cemetery for criminals, a lunatic asylum, and an orphanage for abandoned infants. All this made a lasting impression on the young Dostoevsky, whose interest in and compassion for the poor and oppressed tormented him.

He started to write fiction in late 1844. In 1845, his first work was met with great acclaim and he became a literary celebrity at the age of 24. However, Tsar Nicholas I, after seeing the Revolutions of 1848 in Europe, was harsh on any sort of underground organization and in 1849 Dostoevsky was arrested and imprisoned for being a part of a liberal, intellectual group. He was sentenced to death. After a mock execution, in which he stood outside in freezing weather waiting to be shot by a firing squad, Dostoevsky's sentence was commuted to four years with hard labour in Siberia. Dostoevsky said of this, "From dusk to dawn it was impossible not to behave like pigs." After his ordeal he abandoned 'Western' ideas and began to pay greater attention to traditional Russian values.

After much heartbreak and disappointment, Dostoevsky met Anna Grigorevna Snitkina, a twenty-year old stenographer. Shortly before they married, his writing method changed; he dictated *The Gambler* to her. After this Dostoevsky became acclaimed all over Russia as one of her greatest writers and was hailed as a prophet, almost as a mystic. Forty thousand mourners attended his funeral. To this day his work influences a wide variety of writers.

If you wish to glimpse
inside a human soul
and get to know a
man, don't bother
analyzing his ways of
being silent, of talking,
of weeping, of seeing
how much he is moved
by noble ideas; you will
get better results if
you just watch him
laugh. If he laughs
well, he's a good man.

Fyodor Mikhailovich Dostoevsky
1821–1881

## Johann Wolfgang Goethe (later von Goethe)
## 1749–1832

Goethe, (pronounced Ger-tuh), was from a region that today is part of Germany. He was a multi-talented all rounder: poet, novelist, dramatist, humanist, scientist, theorist, painter and, for ten years, Chief Minister of State of the Duchy of Weimar.

The author of *Faust* and *Theory of Colours* he was one of the key figures in German literature and the Weimar Classicism movement in the late 18th and early 19th centuries. He inspired Darwin with his independent discovery of the human intermaxillary jaw bones and focus on evolutionary ideas. He is widely considered to be one of the most important thinkers in Western culture, and is often cited as one of history's greatest geniuses.

Men show their character in nothing more clearly than by what they think laughable.

Johann Wolfgang von Goethe 1749–1832

# LAUGH

## *To Build Happiness*

## Seneca (Lucius Annaeus Seneca)
## 4 BC–AD 65

A Roman philosopher, statesman, dramatist, and humorist of the Silver Age of Latin literature, Seneca was born in Córdoba, Hispania. His older brother, Gallio, became proconsul at Achaia where he encountered the apostle Paul about AD 52.

Seneca established a successful career as an advocate. When he was about 37, he was nearly killed as a result of a conflict with the Emperor Caligula, who only spared him because he believed the sickly Seneca would not live long anyway.

In 41, Emperor Claudius's wife Messalina, persuaded him to banish Seneca to Corsica on a charge of adultery with Julia Livilla. In AD 49, Claudius' new wife, Agrippina, had Seneca recalled to tutor her son, Nero. On Claudius' death in 54, Agrippina secured the recognition of Nero as emperor over Claudius' son, Britannicus, and Seneca acted as Nero's advisor for eight years from then on.

In 65AD Seneca had a really bad day. He was accused of being involved in a plot to kill Nero. Having escaped an attempt on his life, he went home to commit ritual suicide. He chose to cut his wrists. Unfortunately his diet caused the blood to flow slowly, causing pain instead of a quick death so he took poison given to him by a friend, but it didn't work. He dictated to a scribe, and then jumped into a hot pool to make the blood flow faster. Tacitus wrote in his *Annals of Imperial Rome* that Seneca died from suffocation from the steam rising from the pool. Poor Seneca, some days you just can't win!

Another, who having offended the Emperor, (Nero, who famously fiddled while Rome burned) had to commit suicide! By all accounts he made a rather poor job of it. Just as well, then, that he believed that it's better to treat life as a comedy than a tragedy. A botched suicide is too painful to contemplate if you take it seriously. It plays much better as farce.

It better befits us to laugh at life than to lament over it.

Seneca (Lucius Annaeus Seneca) 4 BC–AD 65

We've all known people who only have to walk into a room to lighten the atmosphere and brighten the spirits of everyone in it.

When this happens naturally it is indeed a gift but it is also something that can be cultivated by conscious choice. What a great reputation to have!

The person who can bring the spirit of laughter into a room is indeed blessed.

Anonymous

## Dr Madan Kataria

An Indian doctor, Madan is popularly known as "The Merry Medicine Man of India" and "The Guru of Giggling".

In 1995 while writing an article entitled *Laughter - The Best Medicine*, for a health magazine, he was so struck by the medical evidence he amassed to prove the cliché that he was inspired to start a Laughing Club. He founded a worldwide movement through which he shares his pioneering techniques of group laughter based on yoga.

Dr Kataria qualified as a medical physician and practiced medicine in Mumbai, India for 20 years. He was previously a registrar specialising in cardiology at Jaslok Hospital and Research Centre, Mumbai.

The Laughter Club concept is widely recognised and Dr. Kataria travels the world advising on the health benefits of laughter to the public, businesses and governments. I was privileged to study with him and due to his unremitting efforts, there are literally thousands of Laughter Clubs around the globe.

The whole world is full of seriousness. As a child one is asked by one's parents over and again, "When will you become serious?" As an adult if you want to be joyful at times, people will say, "Don't behave like a child! Life is serious, death is serious."

There is a lot of seriousness in hospitals and religious places. There is no laughter at workplaces and newspapers and television programmes are continually bombarding us with bad news and negative thoughts, which make people feel even more insecure.

At a tender age, children are being loaded with information. Instead of basketball they are playing computer games and chess where you need to apply a lot of thought and there is practically no laughter. Already children of today are behaving like young adults. People are becoming more logic-oriented; they look for logic in laughter too. The very essence of laughter is absurdity. Where there is logic there is no laughter.

Dr Madan Kataria

## Kate Hull Rodgers

Canadian born, but now resident in Britain, Kate is a speaker, author, media presenter, seminar leader and coach. She is a leading international authority on the strategic use of humour in the workplace.

She has pioneered work in the fields of laughter therapy, stress management, communication and networking. For the past 18 years her advice has been sought by governments, health organisations and businesses in 29 countries, on five continents.

Kate has been resident expert for ITV's Job Finder, a business journalist, a presenter for BBC Radio, an award winning comedienne and playwright. Her work and personal story of mental health recovery are the subject of the ITV documentary *Laughter is the Best Medicine*. Her first business book *Pearls of Bizdom* outlines how businesses can go from grit to great!

In today's stressed out, target driven world, if you wait for reasons to laugh, you just won't find enough of them. Instead, laugh First - on purpose - and you will start to find more things to laugh about. You will lighten up your perspective on things and find the lighter side. With Humourobics we do not laugh because we are happy. We are happy because we laugh.

Kate Hull Rodgers

## Samuel Johnson, LL.D.
## 1709–1784

Often referred to simply as 'Dr. Johnson', he was one of England's greatest literary figures: a poet, essayist, biographer and often considered the finest critic of English literature. He was also a great wit and prose stylist whose witticisms are still frequently quoted today.

The biography, *Life of Johnson* (1791) by his friend James Boswell was revolutionary. It is still often said to be the greatest biography yet written and has much to do with Johnson's enduring reputation. In 1755 his *Dictionary Of The English Language* was published. He had worked for eight years to complete the book. It cost £4/10s (£300 today) and he was paid £1,575 (around £100,000 today). It wasn't the first dictionary to be published, but it secured his position as a literary lion and is the basis of the dictionaries that we use today. For instance 1,700 of Johnson's definitions remain in the Oxford English Dictionary.

Among students of philosophy, Dr. Johnson is perhaps best known for his refutation of Bishop Berkeley's idealism. Despite his formidable literary powers it is endearing to know that words sometimes failed him. During a conversation with Boswell, Johnson became infuriated at the suggestion that Berkeley's idealism could not be refuted. In his anger, Johnson powerfully kicked a nearby stone and proclaimed, of Berkeley's theory, that, "I refute it *thus!*"

Mirth is like a flash of lightning that breaks through a gloom of clouds and glitters for the moment. Cheerfulness keeps up a daylight in the mind, filling it with steady and perpetual serenity.

Samuel Johnson 1709–1784

## J.M. Barrie (Sir James Matthew Barrie, 1st Baronet, OM) 1860–1937

The British novelist and dramatist is best remembered for creating *Peter Pan*, the boy who refused to grow up. Barrie, whose marriage was childless, became a surrogate father to the Llewelyn Davies boys when their father died and, when they were orphaned, he became their guardian. They were part of the inspiration for this enduring and magical tale. *Finding Neverland* (Johnny Depp, Kate Winslet) is a semi-fictional movie about this story.

He was born to Scottish weavers, the ninth child of ten and had a difficult childhood. His father had no relationship with his children and when James was six, David, his mother's favourite, died in a skating accident on the eve of his 14th birthday. His mother never recovered from the loss and cruelly she too ignored James. When he entered room, she would always say, "David, is that you? Could it be you?" and then, "Oh, it's only you." Apparently she found comfort in the fact that her dead son would remain a boy forever, never to grow up and leave her. This had a profound impact on James. He was mentally scarred with the notion that growing up was wrong, and stopped growing at five feet. It is thought he suffered from psychogenic dwarfism. It is easy to speculate that elements of *Peter Pan* derive from his complex childhood as well as admire the positive use of his own grief to bring joy to others.

Barrie wrote a number of works for the theatre. Notable successes included *Quality Street* and *The Admirable Crichton*. In 1924 he specified that the copyright of *Peter Pan* should go to the nation's leading children's hospital, Great Ormond Street Hospital in London.

Those who bring
sunshine to the lives
of others cannot
keep it from
themselves.

J.M. Barrie 1860–1937

# LAUGH

*To Cope With Pain*

## Dr Joel Goodman

One of the heroes of the Laughter Movement, Joel is the Founder (in 1977) and Director of The HUMOR Project, Inc.: the first organisation in the world to focus full-time on the positive power of humour. Its aim is to help people get more 'smileage' out of their lives and jobs by applying the practical, positive power of humour and creativity.

As a recipient of the International Lifetime of Laughter Award, Joel takes his work very seriously and himself very lightly. The HUMOR Project has sponsored 51 international humour conferences, operates the HUMOResources mail-order and on-line bookstore, and has made presentations to more than three million people around the world on the positive power of humour in everyday life and work. Their pioneering work has been featured in more than 4500 television and radio shows, newspapers and magazines, in over 150 countries.

Humour is laughter made from pain—not pain inflicted by laughter.

Dr Joel Goodman

## Elbert Hubbard
## 1856–1915

American writer, publisher, artist, and philosopher, Hubbard was an influential exponent of the Arts and Crafts Movement. Most famous for his essay *A Message to Garcia*, he led a distinguished life, which was enhanced by his uniquely distinguished death.

When the Titanic sank in 1912 he was so moved by the story of Mr & Mrs Isadore Straus that he saluted them in print. Mrs Straus had refused a 'Women and children first' place in the lifeboats saying, "I will not leave my husband. All these years we've travelled together, and shall we part now? No, our fate is one."

Hubbard wrote, 'I envy you that legacy of love and loyalty left to your children and grandchildren. The calm courage that was yours all your long and useful career was your possession in death. You knew how to do three great things—how to live, how to love and how to die … to pass out, as did Mr and Mrs Straus, is glorious. Few have such a privilege. Happy lovers, both; in life they were never separated and in death they are not divided.'

In an amazing coincidence, three years later Elbert and Alice Moore Hubbard (who was a noted suffragist) went down on the Lusitania together. A survivor wrote to their son, 'Neither appeared perturbed in the least … As I moved to the other side of the ship, in preparation for a jump when the right moment came, I called to him, "What are you going to do?" He just shook his head, while Mrs. Hubbard smiled and said, "There does not seem to be anything to do." Then he did one of the most dramatic things I ever saw done. He simply turned with Mrs. Hubbard and entered a room on the top deck, the door of which was open, and closed it behind him. It was apparent that his idea was that they should die together, and not risk being parted on going into the water.'

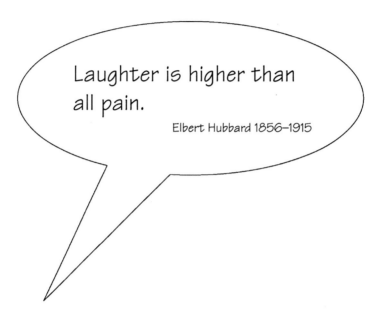

Laughter is higher than all pain.

Elbert Hubbard 1856–1915

## Percy Bysshe Shelley
## 1792–1822

As an English Romantic Poet, Shelley was widely considered to be among the finest lyrical poets of the English language. His unconventional life celebrating republicanism, atheism, vegetarianism, free love and uncompromising idealism, combined with his strong sceptical voice, made him a notorious and much denigrated figure during his life.

However, he became the idol of the next two or three generations of poets, including the major Victorian and Pre-Raphaelite poets Robert Browning, Alfred Tennyson, Dante Gabriel Rossetti, Algernon Charles Swinburne. He was also admired by such as Karl Marx, George Bernard Shaw and William Butler Yeats. He is famous for his association with contemporaries John Keats and Lord Byron; an untimely death at a young age was common to all three. He was married to the famous novelist Mary Shelley, author of Frankenstein, and wrote the introduction to the 1818 edition.

Shelley was the son of Sir Timothy Shelley, MP, and educated at Eton and Oxford University. The plan was for him to inherit his father's seat in Parliament when he was twenty-one. Having developed a strong hatred of tyranny while at Eton, Shelley began reading books by radical political writers and he was expelled from Oxford for writing *The Necessity of Atheism* in which he attacked the idea of compulsory Christianity.

He followed this up by eloping to Scotland with Harriet Westbrook, a sixteen-year old daughter of a coffee-house keeper causing a dreadful scandal. His father never forgave him.

He became deeply involved in radical politics and met the radical writer William Godwin and his wife, Mary Wollstonecraft, the author of *Vindication of the Rights of Women*. Shelley also renewed his friendship with Leigh Hunt, the young editor of *The Examiner*. In 1814 Shelley fell in love and eloped with Mary, the sixteen-year-old daughter of William Godwin and Mary Wollstonecraft. For the next few years they travelled in Europe.

In 1822 Shelley, moved to Italy with Leigh Hunt and Lord Byron where they published the journal *The Liberal*. The first edition sold 4,000 copies and by publishing it in Italy they avoided prosecution in Britain. Soon afterwards, while going to meet Leigh Hunt, Shelley was lost at sea.

Shelley is quite right about laughter. True laughter is when we take our pain and play with it. I hope his father knew how to do that...!

Our sincerest laughter with some pain is fraught;

Percy Bysshe Shelley 1792–1822

# LAUGH

*To Nourish Your Spirit*

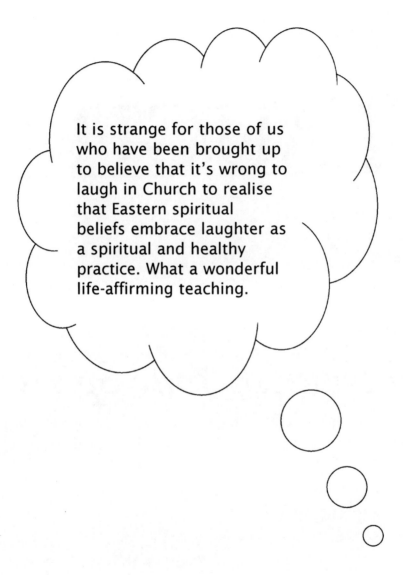

It is strange for those of us who have been brought up to believe that it's wrong to laugh in Church to realise that Eastern spiritual beliefs embrace laughter as a spiritual and healthy practice. What a wonderful life-affirming teaching.

Time spent
laughing
is time spent
with the Gods.

Japanese Proverb

## The Koran (Qur'an)

The Qur'an is the central religious text of Islam. Muslims believe the Qur'an to be the book of divine guidance and direction for mankind. In its original Arabic it is considered to be the literal word of God revealed to Muhammad over a period of twenty-three years as God's final revelation to humanity. Muslims regard the Qur'an as a continuation of other divine messages that started with those revealed to Adam - regarded in Islam as the first prophet - and including the Torah, the Psalms and the Gospel in between.

The Qur'anic text assumes familiarity with many events from Jewish and Christian scriptures, retelling some of these events in distinctive ways and referring obliquely to others. It rarely offers detailed accounts of historical events; the Qur'an's emphasis is typically on the moral significance of an event, rather than its narrative sequence.

The verses were originally memorized by Muhammad's companions, as Muhammad recited them, with some being written down by one or more companions on whatever was at hand, from stones to pieces of bark.

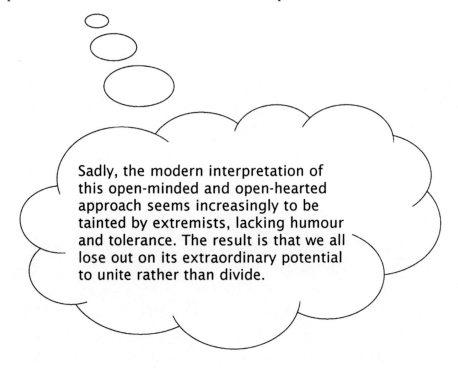

Sadly, the modern interpretation of this open-minded and open-hearted approach seems increasingly to be tainted by extremists, lacking humour and tolerance. The result is that we all lose out on its extraordinary potential to unite rather than divide.

He deserves
Paradise who
makes his
companions
laugh.

The Koran (Qur'on)

# Martin Luther
## 1483–1546

Luther was a German monk, priest, professor, theologian, and church reformer. His teachings inspired the Reformation and deeply influenced the doctrines and culture of the Lutheran and Protestant traditions and, as such, was responsible for completely changing the course of Western civilization. Since my impression is that there is a distinct joylessness about everything he influenced it is good to know how pro-laughter he was!

Thanks to the recently developed printing press, his writings were widely read and influenced many Reformers and thinkers, helping to create a variety of Protestant traditions in Europe and elsewhere. Luther's hymns, including his best-known *A Mighty Fortress is Our God,* inspired the development of congregational singing within Christianity.

His marriage in 1525, to Katharina von Bora reintroduced the practice of clerical marriage within many Christian traditions. Today, nearly seventy million Christians belong to Lutheran churches worldwide, with some four hundred million Protestant Christians tracing their history back to Luther's reforming work. That's quite a legacy!

If you're not allowed to laugh in heaven, I don't want to go there.

Martin Luther 1483–1546

## George MacDonald
## 1824–1905

Though no longer a household name, the Scottish author, poet, and Christian minister's works (particularly his fairy tales and fantasy novels) have inspired deep admiration in such notable writers as W. H. Auden, J. R. R. Tolkien, and Madeleine L'Engle. C. S. Lewis wrote that he regarded MacDonald as his 'master'. G. K. Chesterton cited *The Princess and the Goblin* as a book that had 'made a difference to my whole existence'. Elizabeth Yates wrote of *Sir Gibbie* that 'it moved me the way books did as a child ... Now and then a book is read as a friend, and after it, life is not the same ... *Sir Gibbie* did this to me.'

Even Mark Twain, who initially despised MacDonald, became friends with him and there is some evidence that Twain too was influenced by MacDonald.

MacDonald grew up in an atmosphere of Calvinism but never felt comfortable with some aspects of Calvinist doctrine with a particular distaste for the Calvinist idea that God's electing love is limited to some and denied to others.

It is the heart that is not
yet sure of his God that
is afraid to laugh in His
presence.

George MacDonald 1824–1905

I've always liked the way the Japanese think—they have a way of putting things that gets right to the heart of the matter.

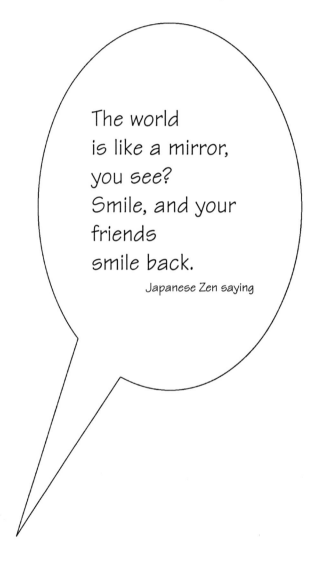

The world
is like a mirror,
you see?
Smile, and your
friends
smile back.

Japanese Zen saying

# In Conclusion

## Why laugh?

If you ever wondered just how laughter could improve your life and reduce stress then take a look below at how and why you would benefit from incorporating more laughter into your life …

## Number 1 - Laugh so much that you nearly fall over.

OK, not quite that bad, but have you ever really let go and just laughed for all you were worth? When you laugh you lose muscle control because laughter has a profoundly relaxing effect on the muscles.

Muscles throughout the body tense and relax during laughter in exactly the same way as in stress reduction techniques such as yoga. So if you laugh with your whole body you are in effect giving yourself a laughter workout.

## Number 2 - Laugh so your sides ache.

When you laugh your diaphragm convulses. This involuntary convulsion of the diaphragm, that is a component of laughter, does two valuable things:

a.  It tones up your muscles - that's why your sides can ache - another workout! and …
b.  Like a bellows it pushes all the stale air out of your lungs, which means that fresh air rushes in to replace it.

## Number 3 - Laughter is good for your blood.

Laughter alters your breathing cycles so that more oxygen is inhaled and toxic carbon dioxide is exhaled. All that inhaled fresh air brings more oxygen into your system, which is what oxygenates the blood.

## Number 4 - Fancy a massage?

When you laugh, the convulsion of the diaphragm causes it to push against your internal organs. This causes a beneficial shake-up and increased blood flow to your internal organs (they like that!).

## Number 5 - More exercise with mirth.

Did you ever feel exhausted from a bout of hearty laughter? That is because laughter acts on your body like exercise. According to Dr. William Fry at Stanford University, "One minute of laughter is equal to 10 minutes on the rowing machine."

## Number 6 - Chuckle to relieve the pressure.

Laughter raises your blood pressure just long enough to increase oxygen and blood supply to tissues and then it reduces. There is compelling evidence to show that regular hearty laughter can permanently reduce your blood pressure—with no side effects. Also, your temporarily increased blood pressure sends an increased volume of blood coursing faster round your body which beneficially expands and energises the whole cardio-vascular system.

## Number 7 - A natural high.

Laughter makes the world seem bright. Endorphins are what make you feel as if the world is a sunnier place. If you ever experienced the 'Runner's High' you may know that endorphins are credited with being our natural source of pain killers and the feel-good factor. The science is young, however, and there is some doubt that it is actually endorphins that are responsible. If it feels good I don't care what they call it, I just enjoy the effect. If you want more scientific detail consult wonderful, wonderful Wikipedia.

## Number 8 - Boost your immune system.

Ontario's Waterloo University recently established that exposure to laughter improves immune system functioning and produces significant rises in the body's natural defences. Chronically low antibody levels produce greater likelihood of future disease. It is particularly intriguing that in this study those classified as having a good sense of humour, given something to laugh at, experienced the greatest rises in antibody levels.

Your immune system is boosted by increasing your levels of:
a) infection-fighting T-cells,
b) disease-fighting proteins called Gamma interferon and
c) B-cells, which produce disease-destroying antibodies, laughter boosts the immune function.

## Number 9 - Give yourself a laughter facial.

Apart from the fact that a smiling or laughing face is naturally many, many times more attractive than one with a neutral expression, laughter increases blood flow to the face and it responds by taking on a rosy glow. It also gives the facial muscles a good work out which tightens everything up.

## Number 10 - Relax and enjoy.

Dr Lee Berk and Dr. Stanley Tan at Loma Linda University have shown that 30 minutes of 'mirthful laughter' (watching a funny movie as opposed to a pleasant one) decreases the cortisol levels in the blood by up to 87%.

This is good because cortisol, like adrenalin, is great for you in emergencies but only in short bursts. Chronic stress occurs when your body doesn't get a chance to return to normal. Prolonged levels of cortisol in the blood stream can create grave consequences, including:

- Reduced thyroid function
- Reduced mental performance
- Blood sugar imbalances
- Reduced bone density
- Decrease in muscle tissue
- Increase in abdominal fat ('apple' pattern)
- Lowered immune function and inflammatory response
- Raised blood pressure.

For healthy cortisol levels it is necessary to enable the body's relaxation response to operate each time the fight or flight response occurs. Laughter is nature's built-in Reset Button.

**Number 11 - Fight depression with a smile.**

Recent research has established that electrical brainwave patterns of the right and left hemisphere of the brain tend to co-ordinate more when we find something humorous and laugh.

This is important because of evidence that depression is accompanied by low co-ordination in brain wave patterns between the two sides.

It has been established with biofeedback and the observation of brainwaves whilst meditating, that the mere act of smiling internally reverses the stress response in our neuro-endocrine system and stimulates our brainwave pattern into deep healing and longevity.

# So.... Why *not* laugh?

# Bibliography

If you are interested in finding out more about the fascinating subject of how Laughter impacts on your Health, Happiness and Wellbeing I list below some books and articles to investigate:

An Anatomy of an Illness by Norman Cousins

Laughter Therapy: How to Laugh About Everything in Your Life That Isn't Really Funny by Annette Goodheart Ph.D., M.F.T

Taking Laughter Seriously by John Morreall

Laughter from Heaven by Barbara Johnson

Gesundheit!: Bringing Good Health to You, the Medical System, and Society through Physician Service, Complementary Therapies, Humor, and Joy by Patch Adams and Maureen Mylander

Laughing Matters, by Joel Goodman

Laugh For No Reason by Madan Kataria

Laughter: A Scientific Investigation by Robert R. Provine

Heart, Humor and Healing by Patty Wooten

Shift Happens!: Powerful Ways to Transform Your Life by Robert Holden

Pearls of Bizdom: How to Go from Grit to Great by Kate Hull Rodgers

# Index

# About the Authors

## Kit Hammond Stapely

In 1998 Kit defied both her doctors and a disastrous life-situation by deciding not to die of aggressive 'incurable' cancer after all! Today, happily remarried and cancer-free, she lives on The River Thames in a converted barge and relishes the privilege of counting certain rather distinguished swans among her friends. She has trained as a Laughter Leader with Dr. Madan Kataria, and as a Laughter Coach and is a member of the Laughter Network. She uses the power of Laughter in every capacity of her life including her work as a Health Creation mentor and Love Yourself, Heal Your Life teacher. Kit's website is: www.miraclesdohappen.org.uk.

## Rhonda Blunden

Rhonda was the only girl on an all-male course when she did her Engineering degree. Her unlikely route to Enlightenment began when she noticed that she got a lot more help from her fellow students when she'd had her highlights done. Eventually the importance of having fun with your work led her from conventional corporate Training and Market Research work into roads less travelled. She trained to become a Reiki Master, N.L.P. Practitioner and a Laughter Coach and opened a Wellness Centre to enable others to live fully. She was initiating original work in the realm of Corporate Wellness. She had much the world needed and is sorely missed.

## Alice Gleadow

Laughter brought Alice and Kit together. When Kit mentioned to a friend at a Laughter Network meeting that she was looking for the right illustrator for this book he suggested his girlfriend could do the job. Alice turned out to be the perfect person. Although she now lives near Brighton, Alice studied illustration at Kingston University not far from where the St Petroc is moored. Her illustration works include commissions for Conde Nast. You can see more of her illustrations at www.alicegleadow.com.

978-0-595-43522-7
0-595-43522-X

Printed in the United Kingdom
by Lightning Source UK Ltd.
125245UK00002B/76-498/A